Austin Travel Guide

Sightseeing, Hotel, Restaurant & Shopping Highlights

Laura Dawson

Table of Contents

Austin

Austin is the capital of the state of Texas and the thirteenth most populous city in the United States. It was settled in the 1830s and has grown steadily since then, and now boasts nearly two million people in the metropolitan area with 800,000 of those people living inside the Austin city limits.

Austin is a city that is full of lights and sounds for those who love city breaks, but also offers beautiful scenery and outdoor adventures for the nature lovers. There is something for everyone. With almost 2,500 hours of sunshine every year, Austin is the place to go if you long for sunny skies.

Culture

Austin is known as "The Live Music Capital of the World" and musicians can be found performing in stores, on the sidewalks, or in one of the two hundred music venues in the city. So grab a drink, get comfortable, and enjoy the soothing music. Most of the music that is popular in Austin has roots in the African American tradition, and include genres such as Blues, Jazz, and hip-hop.

There are also many different Asian cultures that have a strong influence on the area. These cultures have left their mark on various neighborhoods and make up some of the most highly rated restaurants in the area. Austin also prides itself in being an LGBT friendly and welcoming community. All of these groups have annual celebrations of their culture that draws in hundreds of outside participants.

Every year, Austin celebrates the Celtic heritage and culture found within the city. With food, drink, and traditional Scottish and Irish music, it's no wonder the Austin Celtic Festival draws in hundreds of participants.

Texas was a part of Mexico until the middle of the nineteenth century and Mexican culture has played a huge role in influencing the culture of Texas. It is probably the most notable culture within Austin.

Location & Orientation

Austin is located in the middle of the state, approximately 350 miles north of South Padre Island at the bottom tip of Texas. Austin is located in the Central Time Zone of North America. Austin covers almost 300 square miles and is 489 feet above sea level.

Austin encourages public transportation and ridesharing and offers public transportation on the MetroBus and the MetroRail.

Single Fare: $1.00
Single Fare Reduced: ¢50
Day pass: $2.00

Seniors over 65, people with disabilities, elementary and secondary school students with valid identification, and military members are eligible for reduced fare. If you plan on being in the area for an extended stay, consider buying a week's worth of day passes for $9.00 or a month's worth of day passes for $30, 50% off the price of 30 day passes when bought individually.

In 2011, Austin made it to the list of the Top 50 Walkable Cities, coming in at number 31. If you find yourself with some time to spare and the weather is nice, consider walking to your next destination! Walking is a great way to stay within your budget when you're traveling. Biking is another great option for a means of transportation, so check with your hotel or a nearby park to see if they offer bike rentals. Austin also has coordinated rideshare programs for carpooling.

Climate & When to Visit

Austin's climate is categorized as a humid subtropical climate, meaning the summers are hot. The high temperatures in the summer are usually in the upper 90s and relatively dry. The hottest day on record in Austin, Texas was September 5th, 2000 when the temperature reached 112°F.

The winters are usually very pleasant; the average high temperature in December is 61°F. Only rarely does the temperature dip below freezing and the minimum temperature usually stay above 45°F.

The rainiest season is in the spring, so if you are planning on taking in the sights of Austin in the spring, make sure to bring an umbrella! Sometimes, rain showers turn into thunderstorms, but the actual city very rarely sees any tornado activity. The fall months also receive a decent amount of rain, but without the strong thunderstorms. The summer and winter are relatively dry, and snow is incredibly rare.

If you are looking to go to Austin for a hot, sun filled vacation, travel during the summer months. If you are looking for a relaxing break in the winter, Austin is a warm and dry vacation destination that will offer you the tranquility you are looking for. No matter when you travel, there will always be exciting things to do and see in Austin.

Sightseeing Highlights

Ghost Tours

Phone: 512.853.9826
Website: www.austinghosttours.com

Walking Tours: $20.00
Trolley Tours: $25.95
Ghost Investigation: $65.00

For those who love the paranormal, this is a must during your time in Austin. No matter if you are a firm believer or not sure at all about the paranormal world, Austin Ghost Tours will provide an exciting adventure, and hopefully an adventure you will never forget.

The walking tours go through historical downtown Austin is a mixture of paranormal encounters and the history of those who are allegedly haunting the buildings or locations. The trolley tours are similar to the walking tours, with the comfort of riding instead of walking. Both of these tours last for about an hour and a half. These tours allow you access to some of the most haunted buildings in the area.

For the avid ghost hunter, a three hours investigation with professional paranormal scientists may end up being the highlight of your trip. The Ghost Investigation allows you to help discover who the spirits are and where they are located, utilizing the help of paranormal equipment.

Tours continue despite the weather, so feel free to bring an umbrella. While the walking tour is both stroller and wheelchair accessible, Austin Ghost Tours suggests parents use discretion with children under the age of 10. Austin Ghost Tours has been scaring residents and tourists alike for the past ten years.

Haunted Hearse Tours & the Museum of the Weird

Tours begin and end at 701 W 51st Street, Austin, TX
Phone: 512-632-8693

General Admission Rates: $35.00
Tours begin at 8:00 pm and 11:00 pm nightly.

Austin Haunted Hearse Tour takes you to fifteen locations in Austin that have reported paranormal activity. During the two hour tour, you are driven through Austin in a Cadillac hearse that has been converted into a limousine. Tours are much more intimate than the tours with the Austin Ghost Tours, with between two to six people per tour.

For an additional $5.00, you can also choose to visit the Austin Museum of the Weird at the end of your tour, saving you $3.00 off of normal admission prices. This museum investigates UFO and extraterrestrial activity, Bigfoot sightings in Texas and the southern United States, and of course, ghostly encounters.

Austin Steam Train

401 E. Whitestone Blvd., Suite A-103
Cedar Park TX
Phone: 512.477.8468
Email: info@austinsteamtrain.org

Austin is a city that is proud of its history, evident by the many historical sites to see while there. The Austin Steam Train offers an interesting perspective into the history of the railroad in Texas and across the United States. This particular railroad was built in the late nineteenth century by the Southern Pacific Railroad Company and was the first railroad in or out of the city.

Ticket prices and hours of operation vary greatly based on the time of the year and the train tour you wish to go on, so the easiest way to buy tickets or to get additional information is to call the Austin Steam Train Association at 512.477.8468. You may also buy tickets and see the train schedule at website: http://www.austinsteamtrain.org. Additionally, any remaining tickets go on sale at the train station an hour and a half before the train leaves.

The Austin Steam Train is a great activity for both children and adults. While the historic train was not designed to be wheelchair accessible, the staff will work with anyone who requires special accommodations due to any kind of disability. If you are in need of special arrangements, contacting the company before the day you arrive will help them to accommodate you better.

Austin Zoo

10808 Rawhide Trail
Austin, TX
Phone: 512.288.1490

Hours
Summer: 9:30 am-6:00 pm
Winter: 10:00 am-5:30 pm
Closed on Thanksgiving and Christmas Day

General Admission Rates:
Adults: $8.00
Students: $6.00
Seniors: $6.00
Military Personnel (With proper identification): $6.00
Children: $5.00
Member Guests: $5.00

Austin Zoo is a zoo that is rather unique. Rather than breeding animals and bringing in more animals, they are dedicated to taking care of the animals that were abandoned by their owners or rescued from neglectful and abusive situations. Right now, the Austin Zoo is home to over 300 animals, both domestic and exotic. There are many species of monkeys, birds, and reptiles, along with big cats such as panthers. Most of the animals have the ability to come right up to the fence, so the Austin Zoo provides a unique opportunity to get up close and personal with the animals.

The admission fee and any donations help the zoo continue their mission of helping these animals. Every year, the zoo brings in nearly 200,000 visitors every year.

The zoo is a great place for all ages, and is stroller and wheelchair accessible. The zoo staff recommends wearing closed toe shoes to avoid any walking injuries while touring the zoo. A walking tour of the zoo usually takes around an hour and a half. The staff also welcomes you to bring your own food and beverages to enjoy while touring the zoo or enjoy in the picnic area.

Austin Duck Tours

209 East 6th Street☐
Austin, TX 78701
512.477.5274

Tour Start Times:
Monday-Tuesday: 2:00pm
Wednesday-Friday: 11:00 am, 2:00 pm
Saturday-Sunday: 11:00 am, 2:00 pm, 4:00 pm

General Admission Rates:
Adults: $29.95
Seniors: $23.95
Students: $23.95
Children (3-12): $15.95
Children Under 2: Free

The Austin Duck Tours are unlike anything else in the city.

This tour will take you around Lake Austin and the city in an unsinkable Hydra Terra vehicle. Hydra Terra vehicles are unique in the fact that they can drive on land and navigate in the water.

This tour will take you to historical spots across the city, both by land and by water. This is an amazing adventure for both children and adults alike, and will definitely be a highlight of your trip. After all, not many people have the opportunity to ride in a Hydra Terra Vehicle!

The Austin Duck Tours staff encourages you to make reservations in order to ensure your spot on the tour on the day you want. This is especially true if you are traveling around a major holiday or during the summer when tourism to Austin is especially high.

Dinosaur Park

893 Union Chapel Road
Cedar Creek, Texas. 78612
Phone: 512.321.6262

General Admission Rate: $7.00
Children under two are free.
Season passes are available for $20.00 per person and are valid for one year after purchase.

Summer Hours
Tuesday-Sunday: 10:00 am-4:00 pm
Winter Hours:
Saturday and Sunday: 10:00 am-:00 pm
Monday-Friday: Reserved for school groups

The Dinosaur Trail at Dinosaur Park is by far the most popular part of the park.

This half-mile trail takes you through a realistic habitat of a dinosaur, complete with life size replicas of dinosaurs that roamed the area hundreds of millions of years ago. You will also see modern day area wildlife while walking through the woods, such as rabbits, lizards, birds, and some pretty cool insects. There are also scavenger hunts and educational opportunities available for children guests. This is definitely a must on your sightseeing list if you have young children.

Texas Capitol Building

112 East 11th Street
Austin, Texas

Hours
Monday-Friday: 7:00 am-10:00 pm
Saturday-Sunday: 9:00 am-8:00 pm

Built in the late nineteenth century, the Texas capitol building is a historically significant building, as well as an amazing piece of architecture. The capitol building and the surrounding acres contain monuments to honor the history behind the city of Austin and the state's government.

While visiting the Capitol building you can decide to show yourself around the capital with the help of some historical information provided by the Visitor's Center. You can also stop into the Visitor's Center to schedule a free tour with one of the building staff.

Inner Space Cavern

4200 S. IH-35
Georgetown, Texas
Phone: 512.931.2283
Toll Free: 877.931.2283

Summer Hours:
Monday- Saturday: 9:00 am-6:00 pm
Sunday: 10:00 am-6:00 pm

Winter Hours:
Monday- Friday: 9:00 am-4:00 pm
Saturday: 10:00 am-5:00 pm
Sunday: 11:00 am-5:00 pm
Closed on Thanksgiving, Christmas Eve, and Christmas
Day.

While on any tours of the cave, you will have the
opportunity to experience the breathtaking beauty that
was formed beneath the earth's surface almost one
hundred million years ago. The tours only cover a few
miles of the total cave. Much of the cave has yet to be
explored, and fossils of prehistoric animals are often
found throughout the cave.

Adventure Tour

Adults: $19.95
Children (4 -12): $11.95
Children (Under 3): Free

The Adventure tour is an hour and fifteen minute tour that is a great place to start if you have never experienced the thrill of walking through caves.

Explorer Tour

Adult: $21.95
Children (4-12): $13.95

This hour and a half long tour is a great choice if you have some experience with exploring caves, but do not want to spend all afternoon in the cave.

Wild Cave Tour

Adults and Children 13+: $100.00
Active members or family of military with proper identification: $80.00

The Wild Cave tour is definitely for those who have had previous experience with caves. It is an extensive four hour tour of the cave.

Children under the age of thirteen are not permitted on this tour. Children who are under the age of 18 must have a parent's signature in order to participate in this tour.

Pioneer Farms

10621 Pioneer Farms Drive
Austin, Texas
Phone: 512.837.1215
Email: farminfo@pioneerfarms.org

Hours:
Friday-Sunday: 10:00 am-5:00 pm

General Admission Rates
Adults: $8.00
Children: $6.00
Children under 2: Free

Pioneer Farm takes you back in time in Texas history and allows you to see how people lived during the 1800s. There are five main attractions to visit while at Pioneer Farms:
1841 Tonkawa Encampment
1868 German Immigrant Farm
1873 Texan Farm
1887 Cotton Planter's Farm
1899 Sprinkle Corner rural village

All of these sites offer an authentic chance to learn and experience the nineteenth century. There is also a barn with contains many friendly animals and many walking trails to explore the entire farm.

Lady Bird Lake

Lady Bird Lake is a manmade lake that was created in 1960. However, just because it is a manmade lake does not mean it lacks for recreational activities! The city of Austin banned the use of motorized water vehicles in Lady Bird Lake, so it is used mostly by canoers and kayakers. Rowing teams also utilize the 470 acre lakes. Swimming in the lake is also not allowed, but sitting on the grass enjoying a picnic by the lake certainly is! Lady Bird Lake is named after Claudia "Lady Bird" Taylor, who was the wife of President Lyndon B. Johnson and the First Lady from 1963-1969.

Lake Travis

Lake Travis is another manmade lake in the area that is fed by the Colorado River. The lake offers over two hundred miles of shoreline perfect for picnicking and camping. Swimming is allowed in this lake, and with a lake that is over two hundred feet deep, many scuba divers as well. Motor boats and fishing is allowed in this lake, and many people enjoy eating the many kinds of bass that swim in the lake, so bring your fishing pole! Fishing poles and canoes are also available for rent.

Zilker Botanical Garden

2220 Barton Springs Rd
Austin, TX
Phone: 512.477.8672

Hours: 7:00 am-5:30 pm

General Admission Rate:
Children under 3: Free
Children (3-12): $1.00
Adults (13-61): $2.00
Seniors (62+): $1.00

The Zilker Botanical Garden was created in 1955 in an effort encourage education and gardening among people of all ages. Today, the gardens are spread out over 30 acres on the bank of the Colorado River and very near the Lady Bird Lake. Over a quarter of a million visitors from all across the United States come to see the Botanical Garden every year. There are hundreds of different kinds of plants and flowers within the garden, providing a breathtaking sight in comparison to the urban city surrounding the Zilker Botanical Garden.

Lady Bird Johnson Wildflower Center

4801 La Crosse Avenue
Austin, TX
Phone: 512.232.0100

Hours:
Tuesday-Saturday: 9:00 am-5:00 pm
Sunday: 12:00 pm-5:00 pm
Monday: Closed

General Admission Rates:
Adults: $9.00
Seniors (65+): $7.00
Students: $7.00
Children (5-12): $3.00
Children under 5: Free

Named for the wife of President Lyndon B. Johnson, the Lady Bird Johnson Wildflower Center showcases all of the native wildflowers of Texas. With two miles of trails, acres upon acres of gardens, and beautiful bodies of water, this wildflower center is perfect for any nature lover. The Butterfly Garden is unique in that is not an enclosed garden, allowing the butterflies to move freely throughout the Wildflower Center. Butterflies are critically important in a wildflower garden, along with bees, because they pollinate the flowers. Without the help of animals that pollinate, wildflowers would not bloom.

Fall Creek Vineyards

1820 County Rd. 222
Tow, Texas
Phone: 325.379.5361

Hours
Monday-Friday: 11:00 am-4:00 pm
Saturday: 11:00 am-5:00 pm
Sunday: 12:00 pm-4:00 pm

Despite the 80 mile drive from Austin, Fall Creek
Vineyards is an excellent destination for a relaxing
afternoon in the sun with your special someone. With
many different varieties of wine to sample made from the
grapes grown on the vineyard, your tour of the vineyards
is sure to be scenic and pleasant.

Museums

The city of Austin is rich in history and learning,
demonstrated by the many museums in the city and the
surrounding area. Museums are a great way to spend a
rainy afternoon or a quiet day without a lot of running
around. These following museums are some of the best
museums in the area.

Austin Children's Museum

201 Colorado Street
Austin, Texas 78701
Phone: 512-472-2499

Hours:
Tuesday- Saturday: 10:00 am-5:00 pm
Sunday: 12:00 pm-5:00 pm

General Admission Rates:
Adult: $6.50
Children (2+ years): $6.50
Children (12- 23 months): $4.50
Children (Under 12 months): Free

The Austin Children's Museum is a great destination if it suddenly rains and you need to entertain your children for the afternoon. This museum has many educational exhibits for children of all ages. The current featured exhibit teaches children about gravity, inertia, and momentum. Permanent exhibits include the Global City, the Funstruction Zone, which features large building blocks to construct whatever the heart desires, and the Rising Star Ranch. The Rising Star Ranch is for children under the age of two and features many different interactive games for you to enjoy with your toddler!

Texas Natural Science Center

2400 Trinity Street
Austin, TX
Phone: 512.471.1604

Hours:
Monday- Thursday: 9:00 am-5:00 pm
Friday: 9:00 am-4:45 pm
Saturday: 10:00 am-4:45 pm
Sunday: 1:00 pm-4:45

The Museum is closed Thanksgiving, Christmas Eve and
Christmas Day, New Year's Eve and New Year's Day,
Easter, and Independence Day.

Admission: Free!

The Texas Natural Science Center is definitely a place to
stop while you are visiting. This museum is educational,
fun, and best of all, completely affordable. The center has
four indoor exhibits and additional outdoor exhibits. This
science center is home to thousands of different fossils.
The Hall of Geology and Paleontology takes you back
hundreds of millions of years ago when dinosaurs and
other animals roamed the earth, a long before the modern
human came around. The hall contains over five hundred
fossils of dinosaurs, other animals, and plants.

The Great Hall shows off the most valuable and rare fossils that the museum owns. One such fossil, the Texas Pterosaur had a wingspan of almost forty feet, much longer than the wingspan of the winged creatures we see flying around today. The Hall of Texas Wildlife showcases fossils of animals that have been found in the area in more recent future, including mammals, birds, and reptiles. The Hall of Biodiversity is a little bit different than the other indoor exhibits. Instead of focusing only on fossils, this hall offers some different educational opportunities about science in general.

Umlauf Sculpture Garden & Museum

605 Robert E. Lee Road
Austin, TX
Phone: 512.445.5582

Hours:
Monday-Tuesday: Closed
Wednesday-Friday: 10:00am-4:30pm
Saturday-Sunday: 1:00pm-4:30pm

General Admission
Adults: $3.50
Students: $1.50
Seniors: $2.50
Children under 6: Free

The sculptures that are featured in this museum are the works of Charles Umlauf. Umlauf was a world famous sculptor in the twentieth century who was an art professor at the University of Texas, Austin. The museum and the garden is run by volunteers who appreciate the life and work of Charles Umlauf and want to share his sculptures with others. The admission charge is definitely affordable, and this museum is perfect for the art lover.

Texas Music Museum

1009 East 11th Street
Austin, TX
Phone: 512.472.8891

Hours:
Monday-Friday: 9:00 am-4:30 pm
Saturday-Sunday: Closed

General Admission Rates:
Free for most exhibits and special events

The Texas Music Museum celebrates the diverse and colorful past and present of music in Texas. Admission to this museum is free, but free will donations are accepted and appreciated to keep the dream of this museum's founders alive. Tours are usually self-guided, but school and private tours by one of the knowledgeable volunteer staff are also offered by contacting the museum at 512.472.8891. This is a perfect destination for the music lover who is in Austin to appreciate the "Live Music Capital of the World"

National Museum of the Pacific War

340 East Main Street
Fredericksburg, TX
Phone: 830.997.8600

Hours:
Monday-Sunday: 9:00 am-5:00 pm

General Admission Rates
Adults: $14.00
Seniors (62+): $12.00
WWII Veterans: Free

Military personnel (with proper identification):
Students: $7.00
Children: $7.00
Children under 6: Free

This museum is entirely dedicated to those who fought in
the military in the Pacific Ocean during World War II.
Fleet Admiral Nimitz, the commander of over two million
men and women in the Pacific Ocean, was born in
Fredericksburg, Texas, so this town was given the honor
of hosting this museum. The funds to build a Japanese
Peace Garden were provided by the Japanese government
in the years after WWII as a symbol of friendship and
peace between the two countries. As a way of thanking
the men and women who served in WWII, the museum
offers free admission to WWII veterans.

French Legation Museum

802 San Marcos Street
Austin, TX
Phone: 512.472.8180

Hours:
Tuesday-Sunday: 1:00 pm-5:00 pm
Monday: Closed

General Admission Rates: $5.00

The French Legation Museum is run by the Daughters of the Republic of Texas and was built in 1956 as a way to promote the history and culture of Texas. This museum consists of a small house and kitchen that are replicas of houses that women would have kept in nineteenth century Texas. There is also a park that is free and open for use by the public. Pets are welcome, as are picnickers, so grab a lunch and enjoy the afternoon after your tour.

State Parks

McKinney Falls State Park

5808 McKinney Falls Parkway
Austin, TX
Phone: 512.243.1643

Open year round from 8:00 am- 10:00 pm.

General Admission Rates:
Adults: $6.00
Children under 12: Free

McKinney Falls State Park is a perfect destination when
you just need a day off from constantly running around.
Visitors to McKinney enjoy fishing, the small, but
nevertheless majestic waterfall, and wading in the small
resulting lake. There are also options for biking,
picnicking, and camping.

Pedernales Falls State Park

2585 Park Road 6026
Johnson City, TX
Phone: 830.868.7304

Hours: Open year round

Adult General Admission: $5.00
Children under 12: Free

The Pedernales Falls State Park is not directly in Austin, but the scenery is worth the drive. Camping and picnicking are popular activities, as well as hiking, biking, and horseback riding. There are many different species of birds living in the park as well, so pick up a checklist of different birds at the park's Main Office.

Swimming and tubing are also popular in the Pedernales River, and when the average high temperature in July is 92°F, the water is certainly refreshing. However, the Pedernales River is infamous for flash floods, so be prepared to leave the river immediately and head to higher ground if the water starts to rise. It's a good idea to check weather alerts frequently when spending time in and around the water.

Bastrop State Park

3005 Highway 21 East
Bastrop, TX
Phone: 512.321.2101

Open year round

Adult General Admission: $4
Children under 12: Free

Bastrop State Park is about a 40 mile drive from Austin, but is another park that is worth it! This State Park contains part of the "Lost Pines", which are thought to be the remnants of a massive prehistoric pine forest. The trees that are in the State Park are protected from further destruction of logging or fire.

Bastrop State Park is also home to the Lost Pines Golf Course, which is the most scenic golf course in the area. The beautiful weather in central Texas ensures the golf course can be utilized year round. Golf carts and pull carts are available for rent. There is also a miniature golf course available for the younger golfers.

As with many State Parks, camping and picnicking are popular activities. The park also rents out canoes, and many enjoy fishing or simply being on the water.

Lockhart State Park

4179 State Park Road
Lockhart, TX 78644-9716
Phone: 512.398.3479

Hours: Open year round

General Admission Rates: $3.00
Kids under 12: Free

Lockhart State Park is located about 40 miles south of Austin. This beautiful state park offers camping, fishing, and picnicking, as well as hiking and a golf course. The golf course is the only state park golf course that is operated by State Park employees. Golf clubs and carts are available for rent at the main office. Lockhart State Park also offers education programs for children and adults. Activities include stargazing and night hikes, bird watching, and conservation programs.

Recommendations for the Budget Traveller

Places to Stay

Austin Motel

1220 South Congress Avenue
Austin, TX
Phone: 512.441.1157
Email: reservations@austinmotel.com

The Austin Motel is a funky little motel in a trendy neighborhood.

Bedrooms that sleep up to two people run for about $110.00 per night, which is much more affordable than some of the higher end hotels in the area. The Austin Motel is on South Congress Avenue, sometimes known as SoCo, which has some of the best places for shopping and food. There are also bars and nightclubs in the area.

Adams House Bed and Breakfast

4300 Avenue G
Austin, TX
512.453.7696
Email: reservations@theadamshouse.com

Considered to be a historic landmark, the Adams House Bed and Breakfast is a popular place to stay. Rooms start at $129.00 per night for two people. Rooms include free Wi-Fi connection, air conditioning and central heat, a hairdryer, and bottled water. There is also an iron and ironing board in the common area, as well as couches to relax on while watching television or a movie. The Adams House also offers a free and organic breakfast from 7:00 am- 9:00 am during the week and starting at 9:00 am on the weekends.

While the Adams House is not in downtown, there are many different things to do in the area. There are many popular restaurants within walking distance, as well as many sightseeing opportunities. This out of the way bed and breakfast is the perfect way to stay while in Austin.

Hostelling International

2200 South Lakeshore Blvd
Austin, TX
Phone: 512.444.2294

If you are really looking for a bargain while staying in the area, a hostel makes a great place to stay. A bed for one night runs a person about $22.00, so this is a great choice if you are traveling alone and have no need for a room for yourself. It's also a great way to budget in general. Sheets are included at this hostel, so no need to bring your own. Hostels provide a great opportunity to meet other travelers to the area.

Hostelling International Austin also is very environmentally friendly, and often hosts events with the city to pick up trash and volunteer in public parks and gardens to keep the city of Austin looking beautiful.

La Quinta Inn Austin

300 East 11th St
Austin, TX 78701
Phone: 512.476.1166

The La Quinta Inn is a very inclusive stay for only $115.00 per night for one room. This Inn boasts an outdoor pool, business center, free Wi-FI connection, fitness center, and is also pet friendly. La Quinta also offers a delicious free breakfast, which includes cereals, waffles, fresh fruit, and all the coffee and juice you can drink.

Americas Best Value Inn

909 E. Koenig Lane
Austin, TX
512.452.4200

Americas Best Value Inn really lives up to its name. Before any discounts, one room is about $62.00 per night. Discounts are available for seniors, military members, and government employees. This inn offers Wi-Fi connection, an outdoor pool, business and meeting areas, an exercise center, laundry services and a continental breakfast.

Places to Eat

Ruby's BBQ

512 West 29th Street,
Austin, TX
Phone: 512.477.1651
Email: info@rubysbbq.com

Founded in 1988, the initial goal of Ruby's BBQ was to offer quality, affordable food for the University of Texas students and the surrounding area. This BBQ restaurant does not only offer quality meat, but soups, salads, and vegetarians options as well. However, most people who visit Ruby's enjoy their brisket, chicken, or ribs.

The meat is cooked in the brick pits that are no longer used in many restaurants. Brick pits require wood as well as a lot of human involvement in the cooking process which many larger restaurants cannot use due to the restricted amount of meat they can cook at one time. Ruby's also makes all of its side dishes on site, so you know your meal is fresh! Entree prices range from $5.00 to $15.00, making Ruby's an unbeatable restaurant.

Sandy's

603 Barton Springs Road
Austin, TX
Phone: 512.478.6322

Hours:
Monday-Sunday: 10:30 am-10:30 pm

Some would say that Sandy's is one of the best kept secrets when it comes to hamburgers. Sandy's is an old fashioned hamburger joint that offers hamburgers, French fries, hot dogs, root beer floats, and custard. The hamburgers are no-nonsense and come with the basic trimmings of a good hamburger. It is not hard to get a great hamburger basket and a drink for less than $5.00.

Casino El Camino

517 East 6th Street
Austin, TX 78701
Phone: 512.469.9330

When you have a late night craving for an amazing burger, Casino El Camino is the place for you as the kitchen in this bar stays open until 1:30 am. Casino El Camino offers burgers, chicken wings, hot dogs, and assorted cold sandwiches. The food has been named the best bar food in Austin and has been featured on the Food Network show "Diners, Drive-ins, and Dives". Even better, no entree on the menu is more than $9.00, and the meat they use in their dishes is from environmentally sustainable, small, local farms.

Java Noodles

2400 East Oltorf Street #14
Austin, TX
Phone: 512.443.5282

Java Noodles is an awesome place to stop when you are craving Indonesian inspired food. The entrees are under $10.00, which is helpful when traveling on a budget. The restaurant also accommodates those who follow vegetarian or vegan diets, as well as offering many entrees for picky children.

El Pollo Regio

6615 Berkman Drive
Austin, TX
Phone: 512.933.9557

Brought to Austin from Mexico in 1995, this marinated chicken has been popular with Texans for years. While the first location was opened in Austin, this restaurant has many different locations in Texas. The prices are surprising considering the amount and quality of food you receive. An order of 16 pieces of chicken, along with two orders of rice, two orders of beans, two orders of tortillas, and salsa only costs a little over $20.00. If you don't need a family size order of food, two pieces of chicken with sides of rice, beans, and tortillas will only set you back about $4.00.

Places to Shop

Flashback Vintage

1805 S 1st Street
Austin, TX
Phone: 512.445.6906

Flashback has been an amazing place to shop since 1982. Flashback is far from your neighborhood thrift store, offering high end and designer vintage clothing.

Flashback accepts vintage pieces in good condition to resell to the public. Shopping 'vintage' is popular among many groups of people today, helps save money, and is quite environmentally friendly. Flashback carries men's and women's clothing that will help you create a look that is all your own. Employees are knowledgeable, helpful, and friendly, and will help you achieve your desired look.

Blue Velvet

217 W. North Loop Blvd
Austin, TX
Phone: 512.452.2583
Email: bvvintage@gmail.com

Monday-Sunday: 11 am-8 pm

Another famous vintage store in the area, Blue Velvet will help you find an outfit for whatever occasion you are shopping for. Blue Velvet makes a point to buy clothing in all different sizes in an effort to cater to all body types. Blue Velvet has men's clothing and shoes, women's clothing and shoes, as well as accessories.

Spring Frost Boutique

5101 Burnet Road
Austin, TX
Phone: 512.467.9100

Hours:
Monday-Saturday: 10:00 am-6:00 pm

Spring Frost Boutique is a great place to shop if you are looking for designer clothing but are not willing to pay designer prices. This boutique offers designer clothing for up to 75% off the designer's asking price, so while the prices may be a little higher than at other stores, the quality of clothing you find there is unbeatable. The staff is knowledgeable and friendly, and will help to whatever extent they are needed. If you are not a fan of shopping, the staff will do the finding for you and bring you different pieces to try on while you relax with a glass of wine in the fitting room. They will also go out of their way to make sure your shopping trip is enjoyable and comfortable.

Big Bertha's Bargain Basement

1050 South Lamar Boulevard
Austin, TX
Phone: 512.444.5908

Big Bertha's Bargain Basement is a great place to shop if you are looking for last season's pieces. You will not pay full price for anything in this store, regardless of whether it is new or used.

Ross Dress For Less

5400 Brodie Ln # 500
Austin, TX
Phone: 512-892-2874

While Ross Dress for Less is a chain store, you will have a unique shopping experience at each store, and the Austin location is no different. Ross carries clothing, accessories, and shoes for men, women, and children. Many of the brands are designer but are sold for half of what they sell for in department stores. Ross also prides itself in being a socially responsible company, treating all of its employees ethically and providing products that have been made in an environmentally sustainable way

Printed in Great Britain
by Amazon